AN ILLUSTRATED TOUR
Color Your Way Through Franklin's History

Mill City Park
and

Courtney Parsons   Heidi Smith

An Illustrated Tour
Color Your Way Through Franklin's History

Library of Congress Control Number: 2022910448

Paperback ISBN: 979-8-9854340-4-0

Book Cover Design: Courtney Parsons

Book Design and Layout: Pamela Marin-Kingsley

Book Editor: Jane Stucker

Book Collaborator: Heidi Smith

Give a Salute! provides publishing services to the author(s) specifications and approval. The author retains all responsibilities and rights to the content of this book.

Contact for More Information:

GIVE A SALUTE!
Laconia, NH
www.giveasalute.com

This book is dedicated to the City of Franklin, its residents, believers and supporters.

Over 100 years ago, Reverend Franklin Ward spoke about his home city. His message still rings true today.

"Yet, the town was destined because of its remarkable water power for an important future. The power of the three rivers, that ceaseless energy, which is renewed every fall of the rain from heaven, had defiled the carelessness of men to lessen its store, and its new citizens should realize that the power which built Franklin, is there to build a still greater Franklin.

- Reverend Franklin Ward, 1892

**Special thanks to Franklin Public Library, the Franklin Historical Society
and the volunteers who made this book possible.**

Meet the Authors

Mill City Park

In the winter of 1968, **Glenn Morrill** volunteered with his father at the Veterans Memorial Ski area in town. He has been involved ever since. For him, his wife, Carolyn, and their boys, volunteering isn't an option but a way of life.

Glenn is a mountain of local knowledge and considers himself a "collector" of local stories and historical photos, which he thoroughly enjoys. It is no coincidence that you will find him all over the city: at his local church, weeding Trestle View Park, biking at Franklin Falls Dam, or whitewater rafting the Winnipesaukee River . . . and he wouldn't have it any other way.

Fun Fact: Glenn was the master chef for the Whitewater Park's first ever fundraiser. Here he can be seen grilling chicken and using a sprayer for his barbecue sauce.

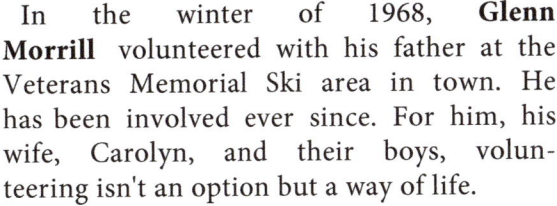

Jo Brown is a 4th generation native of Franklin. She left her city for a full-time active duty career in the United States Air Force and then spent a dozen years in corporate America. She returned to her hometown in 2011, and immediately became involved in helping to bring back the city she knew and loved as a child. In 2015, she opened up The Franklin Cafe, and soon after, Outdoor New England and Vulgar Brewery followed.

Jo is very excited she was able to be part of the great things that have happened in Franklin and, as Franklin's mayor, will continue to help that momentum.

Marty Parichand lives, works and plays in Franklin, New Hampshire. The ongoing joke is that he never leaves town. He founded both Outdoor New England, a gear shop located downtown, and the non-profit Mill City Park, which partnered with the City of Franklin. Together they built New England's white water, utilized 13 acres of unused land to build a community adventure park, and another 18 riverfront acres were put into long-term conservation. Swing by the shop and say, "Hi!" If you talk to Marty, you can probably get him to close up and go surfing.

FRANKLIN, NH
The Three Rivers City

Franklin, New Hampshire, is situated at the confluence of the Pemigewasset and Winnipesaukee Rivers that form the Merrimack River. The town was settled by Anglo-European colonists in 1764, and originally known as "Pemigewasset Village." The name "Franklin" was adopted in 1820, in honor of statesman and founding father Benjamin Franklin. Water power from the falls on the Winnipesaukee River helped it develop as a mill town. It was incorporated as a town in 1828, and then as a city in 1895. Canoeing, kayaking and other water sports are an active part of Frankin's culture.

In this section, we are giving you a quick tour of some sites which are all located close to one another in downtown Franklin. We have also provided descriptions of these notable places. However, the focus of this coloring book is about the other equally amazing sites that are sometimes forgotten about when exploring the Three Rivers City.

Franklin City Hall

Planned and built in 1892, and dedicated on Sept 5, 1893, the Franklin City Hall cost $4,095.07, and 600,000 bricks made in Boscawen, NH, were used in the construction. The building was designed by William Butterfield in the Romanesque Revival style and housed the town offices which included police and water departments, the city court, a theatre and function hall.

Fun Fact: There were 1,200 people in attendance for the dedication ceremony and many more outside.

Franklin Public Library

The library was built in 1903. Andrew Carnegie, an industrialist and philanthropist, gave $15,000 for its construction. "It was from my own early experience that I decided there was no use to which money could be applied so productive. . . as the founding of the public library."

Fun Fact: In addition to funding libraries, Andrew Carnegie paid for thousands of church organs in the United States and around the world.

The Baptist Church of Franklin

The present church was built in 1870, and financed by Walter Aiken, a well-known Franklin businessman. This was the first church that was built on the east side of the river. Then called The First Baptist Church, it united with The Freewill Baptist Church and subsequently was renamed The Baptist Church of Franklin. In 1919, extensive renovations were made using many of the stained-glass windows from The Freewill Church.

Fun Fact: The church still holds services to this day.

Former Franklin High School

The old Franklin High School was completed in 1876, with its first term held that spring and the first class graduating in 1878. A new high school was built in the 1940s in its present location.

Fun Fact: It now also houses SAU 18.

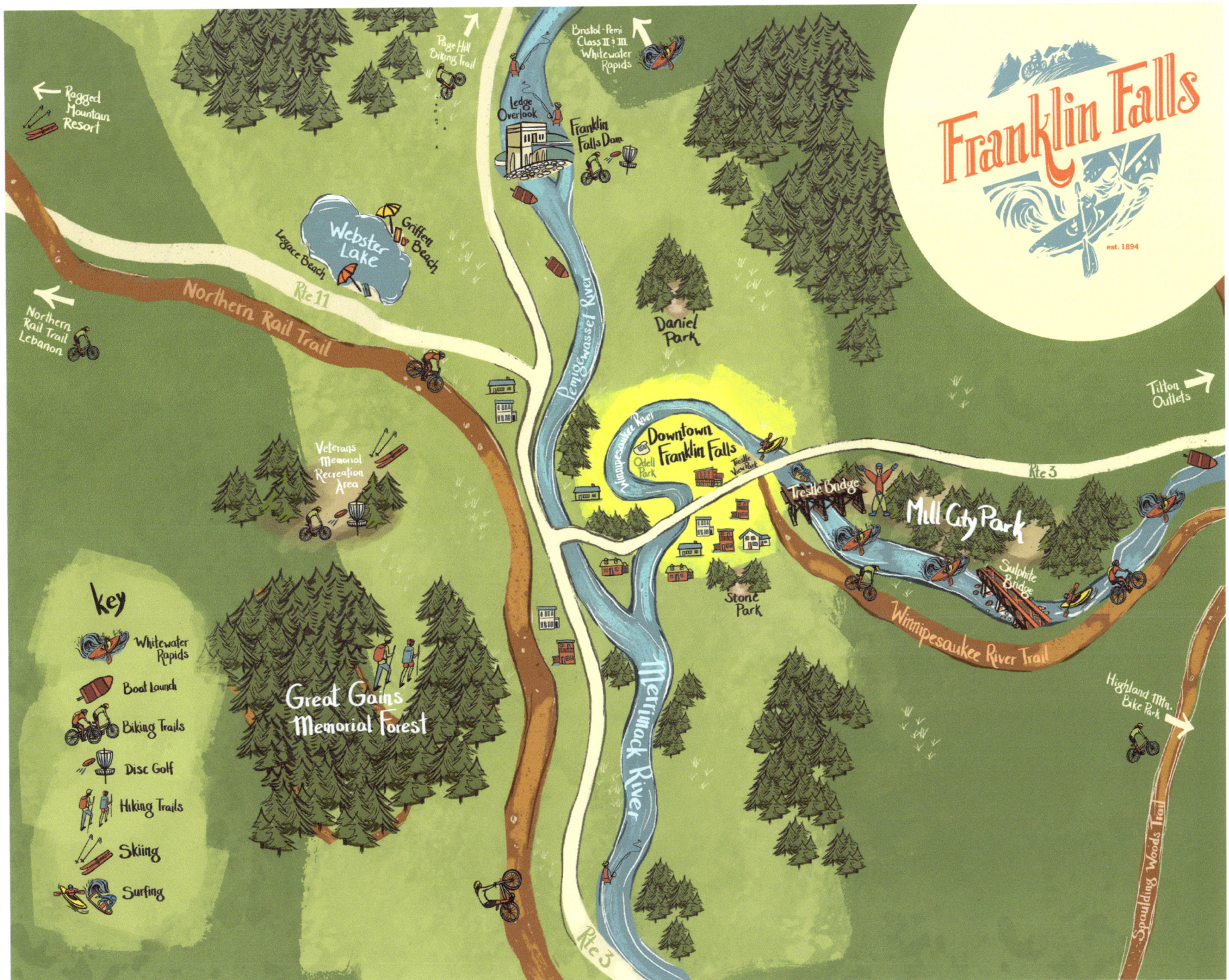

Paper Mill B, J.P. Stevens Mill, and Aiken Mills

Years ago, the river was sheltered from downtown with an abundance of mills using its power. Paper Mill B, owned by the International Paper Company, sat on the south side of the river (in the left of the photo), at the exact location Trestle View Park currently sits. Downstream on the same side of the river was M.T. Stevens Mill, later known as J.P. Stevens Mill. Lastly, across the river was the Aiken Mills. Respectively, these mills made paper woolen products and textiles. These mills also reshaped the downtown corridor and provided the community with opportunity and jobs. Economic vitality came in the form of jobs, as well as the commerce required for Franklin residents' everyday life.

Fun Fact: Trains would travel under the trestle and cross over Central Street to the J.P. Stevens Mill.

Courtesy of the Franklin Historical Society

Sanborn Bridge

Like many locations along the river, standing on the Sanborn Bridge and looking downstream into downtown is totally different from the way it was 15 years ago. Today, Trestle View Park and Whitewater Park greet folks as they enter the downtown Historic District, and the river is totally exposed for visitors and residents to enjoy.

The Sanborn Bridge was built in 1940. The structure is a steel stringer bridge over the Winnipesaukee River on US-3.

Fun Fact: It is also called "The Winnipesaukee River Central Street Bridge."

Courtesy of G. Morrill

Whitewater Park

Free outdoor recreation is Franklin's new calling. With over 150 miles of trails to bike, hike or run, three rivers to paddle and fish, a lake, a ski area, and New England's first whitewater park, many are visiting Franklin each day to explore the outdoors.

The Winnipesaukee River is the reason that Franklin Falls and the Whitewater Park exist. In looking back to Franklin's industrial past, we are able to re-imagine our community's future, and it lies on the riverbanks.

The primary goal of all improvements is simple . . . to connect the community to the river.

Fun Fact: The Winnipesaukee River was once known as Winnipiseogee River.

Courtesy of N. Mason

Franklin Public Library

The Franklin Public Library, funded by Andrew Carnegie, was designed by architect William H. McLean from Boston, Massachusetts. He was well-known for his design of public libraries.

Fun Fact: The Franklin Public Library was built in Carnegie Classical Revival Style and is one of nine Carnegie libraries in New Hampshire.

Courtesy of the Franklin Historical Society

Sulloway House

Construction began on the Sulloway House in 1875, and was completed in 1877. The home was built by Alvah W. Sulloway, an industrialist, and located on a bend in the Winnipesaukee River. He manufactured stockings on the former Elkins Farm in a mill located near the dam on the east side of the river. After several partnerships, A.W. Sulloway became sole owner of the business which flourished under his management. The home itself was a masterpiece of craftsmanship with black walnut walls and a mantle of Italian marble.

Fun Fact: Mr. Sulloway lived in his home for 50 years.

Courtesy of G. Morrill

Sulloway Mills

This mill building was built in 1864, when Frank H. Daniell and Alvah W. Sulloway became partners in the manufacturing of woolen hosiery. The mill was located on the east end of the dam on the Winnipesaukee River. Five years later, Alvah Sulloway bought the building and machines from his partner and became the sole owner of the hosiery business in 1869.

It was a 4-story mill building costing $30,000 to build and was considered the best manufacturing building in Franklin. At this time, the mill was manufacturing 45 dozen hose and 12,000 yards of flannel daily with about 40 employees. The company eventually grew to about 225 employees and operated until 1953.

Fun Fact: After 89 years of manufacturing hosiery, Sulloway Mills closed on April 30, 1953.

Courtesy of G. Morrill

The Franklin Mills

The Franklin Mills started in the current J.P. Stevens/Chinburg Properties location on the Winnipesaukee River around the mid-1860s and produced woolen goods. In 1871, M.T. Stevens leased the mill to make woolen dresses, dying their cloth on-site. M.T. Stevens and Sons was founded in 1813, in North Andover, Massachusetts, by Captain Nathaniel Stevens. In 1850, Nathaniel's son Moses T. Stevens became a partner, and in 1885, the name was changed to M.T. Stevens and Sons. At this time, the company owned a number of mills in the New England area. In 1946, the name changed again to J.P. Stevens and continued to manufacture woolen textiles in Franklin until the operation was moved to North Carolina in the 1970's.

Fun Fact: M.T. Stevens and Sons began in a converted grist mill, producing woolen broadcloth.

Courtesy of G. Morrill

Sulphite Bridge

Sulphite Bridge, also known as the upside-down bridge, was built in 1896. The Franklin and Tilton Railroad line ran across the top of the bridge, and the lower part was covered to protect the trusses from the elements. The bridge is 232 feet long and was named the Sulphite Bridge because sulphite was delivered to the papermills along this railroad line at Franklin Falls. Sulphite was used in the manufacture of paper. This landmark was damaged by fire on October 27, 1980, but is still visible as you walk along the Winnipesaukee trail from downtown Franklin.

Fun Fact: The last train to cross this bridge was in 1976.

Courtesy of G. Morrill

Winnipesaukee River and Paper Mill

This mill was located in what was called Paper Mill Square near Central Street and West Bow Street. It was called Paper Mill C and was started by the Peabody Brothers. It later became part of the International Paper Company (IPC). In 1924, Sulloway Mills bought the land and buildings from IPC so they could acquire the water rights on the west end of the dam to generate electricity to run Sulloway Mills. The buildings were demolished in the late 1920s.

Fun Fact: Franklin was once referred to as the "Paper Mill City."

Courtesy of G. Morrill

The Old Stone Mill

The Franklin Mills Corporation started construction on a 4-story stone mill in 1852, on the Winnipesaukee River, the site of the present Mill City Park. The mill manufactured wool stockings and underwear. On October 24, 1852, the building was being completed when the workers were advised of the death of local orator Daniel Webster. A black band was painted around the top of the chimney in remembrance of the great statesman. On March 13, 1857, a fire destroyed the stone mill and left about half of Frankin residents without jobs.

Fun Fact: It was the first hosiery and underwear mill in New Hampshire and the second hosiery mill in New England.

Courtesy of the Franklin Public Library

Row Houses

This line of white buildings alongside the Winnipesaukee River was called White Row, now part of present-day Mill City Park, in downtown Franklin. These houses were built for the mill workers during the late 1800s. They were taken down when the Franklin Tilton Railroad line was built.

Fun Fact: The immigrants who came to Franklin to work in the mills were mainly French Canadian, Polish or Irish.

Courtesy of the Franklin Public Library

Harry's Mill

The rapid known to kayakers as Coliseum is an odd pairing of history and environment. Mother Nature is actively reclaiming the man-made mill, dam and all associated material back into the landscape and the river corridor.

The rapid is hard and powerful and accurately illustrates why this site was selected for "Harry's Mill" over 150 years ago. It is difficult to imagine so few trees, a road, a dam and a massive mill building sitting on the north side of the river. However, Mother Nature hasn't torn it all down. The wall closest to the river still stands proud among the chaos of the whitewater.

The Winnipesaukee Paper Company actually owned "Harry's Mill" and later sold it to the International Paper Company. Its entire life was spent as a wood pulp mill providing pulp to the other paper mills in the area.

Fun Fact: It was named "Harry's Mill" because Harry W. Daniell was the first superintendent of the facility. Mr. Daniell was a prominent member of the community, being a resident for over six decades and having been mayor of the City of Franklin.

Courtesy of G. Morrill

The Republican Covered Bridge

This bridge was built in 1839, by Boston John Clark and would be the third Republican bridge in this location. The first and second bridges had been damaged or taken out by floods in the Pemigewasset River. This was the first covered bridge at this location in Franklin and cost $7,000 to build. It was a diagonal lattice truss design that was held together with white oak pins made by Herrick Aiken. It took six ox-drawn carloads to deliver the materials to the bridge site where it stood from 1839-1931, when it was replaced with another wooden bridge.

Boston John Clark, who also built many other bridges and dams throughout New England, was a master builder whose only education was a four-year apprenticeship in the building trades in Boston.

Fun Fact: Boston John Clark's constant companion was his 10-foot pole. He was never seen without it.

Courtesy of the Franklin Historical Society

Franklin Hospital

The origins of the Franklin Hospital began in 1900, when a public meeting was held at the Franklin Opera House to discuss the establishment of a public hospital. An estate gift from Mrs. Sally H. Proctor provided the seed funding. A Hospital Aid Society was formed to provide care, clothing, bedding and other supplies for accidents and to continue to encourage the establishment and funding of a public hospital as soon as it was economically feasible.

In the summer of 1907, James Aiken decided to sell his father's house and indicated that the family would prefer to have it used as a hospital. With this bequest, the city purchased the property in 1908. On January 1, 1910, under the guidance of The Franklin Hospital Association, the Franklin Hospital opened.

Fun Fact: In 1967, recognizing the need for growth, Franklin Hospital began expanding the facility. In keeping with the traditions of involving the community, Franklin Hospital reached out and asked, "WHAT'S IN A NAME?" Everyone was allowed to vote and the new name became Franklin Regional Hospital.

Both images courtesy of the Franklin Historical Society

WHAT'S IN A NAME?

☐ Franklin General Hospital

☐ Franklin Tri-County Regional Hospital

☐ Franklin Regional Hospital   Thursday, Oct. 26, 1967

☐ Franklin Community Hospital

Odell Park

Before the area of land now known as the "Three Rivers City," the headwaters of the Merrimack River, the land at the intersection of the Pemigewasset, Winnipesaukee and Merrimack Rivers, was known as "the Crotch." This area was frequented by indigenous people. Present-day Franklin, inhabited by the Abenaki, is just one spot in an expansive area that stretches across the province of Quebec, Canada, as well as Maine, New Hampshire, Vermont, New York and Massachusetts.

Not far from these headwaters is Odell Park where many Native American artifacts, such as tools, tomahawks, weapons, etc., have been found. Odell Park was one of several Indian villages that lined the rivers because of the abundance of fish, a necessary food source for the Native Americans. It is likely that there were nut-bearing trees and berry bushes, and the flat land along the river would have been perfect for farming.

The Abenaki descriptions for these rivers: Pemigewasset, "swift current"; Merrimack, "deep river"; and Winnipesaukee, "land around the lake," are as valid today as when they were when first named.

Fun Fact: Many Native American artifacts are now kept at the Hood Museum of Art at Dartmouth College.

Courtesy of G. Morrill

Central Street

Central Street continues to be the hub of downtown Franklin. Its wide highway lanes and beautiful architecture give it a timeless quality. Just past the building at the far end is the Winnipesaukee River, the site of Mill City Park and New England's first whitewater park. Features in the river that channel the water allow for kayaks to play in the river, and riverside seating provides the public ample viewing space to watch all the action.

Fun Fact: The brick building in front of the tall chimney is the site of present-day Grevior Furniture, a landmark family-owned and operated business in Franklin, NH, since 1932.

Courtesy of the Franklin Historical Society

Buell's Block

Buell's Block has been a long-standing location for apartments and businesses for over 144 years. Built in 1878, it is likely named for George Buell who worked as a supervisor in the Franklin Mills with Walter Aiken. It has been the home of a myriad of businesses over the years, including a cloth remnant shop, shoe store, tobacco store, tattoo parlor and professional offices. Significant renovation of the storefronts began in 2015.

Fun Fact: Currently, Buell's Block houses The Franklin Cafe, Outdoor New England and the Vulgar Brewing Company.

Courtesy of the Franklin Historical Society

J.J. Newberry Co.

J.J. Newberry Co. was a popular five and dime store chain in the 20th century and was a favorite lunch place during its time in Franklin. It was founded in Stroudsburg, Pennsylvania, in 1911, by John Josiah Newberry. J.J. Newberry Co. offered a variety of goods from clothing, toys, and small appliances, as well as a great lunch counter. Children of Franklin in the 1960s will remember shopping for school clothes, toys and candy or sitting at the counter watching the traffic on Central Street. The building was remodeled in the 1960s but eventually closed in the 1990s.

Fun Fact: NH poet, Donald Hall, a former poet laureate of the United States, wrote a short verse, "Beans and Franks," about the closing of the J.J. Newberry Co. store in Franklin.

Courtesy of G. Morrill

Kayak Man

Kayak Man is the result of a community contest to help promote togetherness. As a young boy, Kayak Man had been considering how to show his love for both the outdoors and his community. He was aware that there was a lot of talk about cleaning up the Winnipesaukee River in downtown Franklin and building a whitewater park that would draw in a lot of kayaks. He entered the contest and won!! He became Kayak Man and every day helps show all who pass by how to share a smile, to be excited about life, to stand tall and to care about others.

In his starring role, Kayak Man has worn many hats: a baseball hat for every day, a graduation cap for all our students, a Thanksgiving hat to show thanks for all good things, and a surgical mask throughout the pandemic, along with a heart-shaped "I Love You" sign supporting all our healthcare workers. He's worn a construction cap during the whitewater feature build, and now he's wearing a blue kayak helmet for his trips down the river. Kayak Man is a great symbol of the importance of outdoor recreation for our city, and we can't wait to see what hat he will wear next.

Fun Fact: If you turn Kayak Man sideways, he looks like a kayak.

Courtesy of C. Morrill

Courtney Parsons

Courtney Parsons is an illustrator, graphic designer, and a free-lance artist hailing from Laconia, New Hampshire. Above all, she is a nature admirer and an animal lover, both being prominent themes throughout much of her artistic work. Currently, Courtney resides in Northern Virginia, where she works, attends George Mason University, and lives with her fiancé and cat. Courtney has a deep-rooted fondness for the beautiful Lakes Region, and she considers it an honor to be involved in this project with Heidi and the entire team at Give a Salute!.

Heidi Smith

Heidi Smith is a native of New Hampshire's Lakes Region, where she raised her son and still resides. She has spent the majority of her professional career in the local health care setting, celebrating over 37 years.

Her passion for history has led her to many opportunities, one of which is the coloring book series, *Color Your Way USA*. This began after she noticed Courtney Parsons' online drawing of the Colonial Theatre, which is located in Heidi's hometown. Once she saw the illustration, she knew a coloring book series featuring different historical locations throughout the country needed to be created.

Along with Courtney and the staff of Give a Salute!, Heidi and the team put this concept into design, and they are now collaborating with several nonprofits to help raise money for those organizations as a unique way to preserve and interact with history.

We hope you have enjoyed coloring your way through Franklin's history, and you have also learned a little about its past.

To find out how to color your way through your own community's history, we invite you to contact **Give a Salute!** at **giveasalute@gmail.com**. Also, be sure to check out our website at **http://giveasalute.com**.

www.ingramcontent.com/pod-product-compliance
Lightning Source LLC
Chambersburg PA
CBHW040817120626

46551CB00004B/581